# KEEN TO BE GREEN

Written by Christine Jenkins

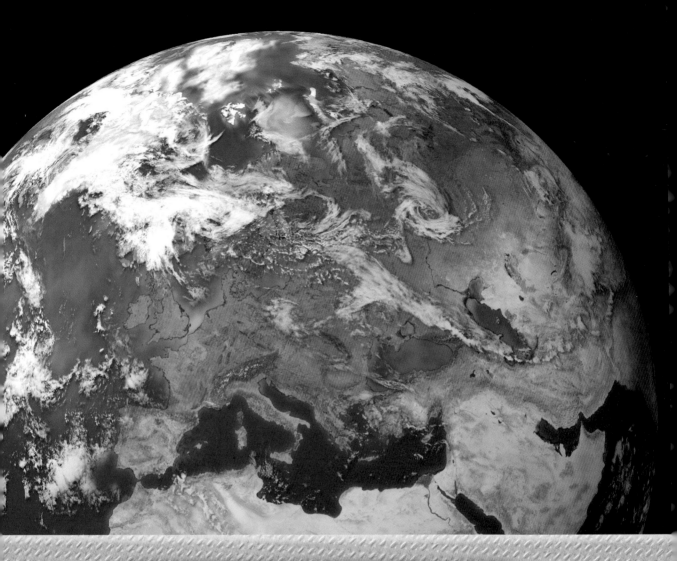

Are you keen to be green?
We can all help to keep the
planet green.

See some things you can do.

Do not let drips go down the drain!
You need to check three things.

**1** Are the taps off?

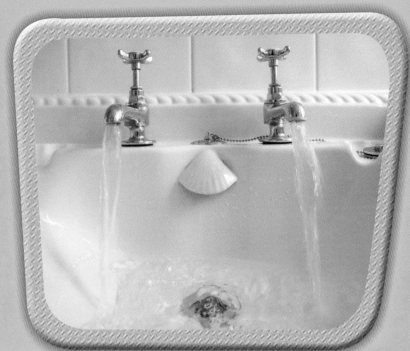

**2** Is the plug in?

**3** No drips from the tap?

Do not dump plastic and tins in the bin. Peelings can go in the compost.

A pond helps to keep things green.
Can you see the bugs and bees?

Keep a bit of land free.

Let some weeds creep in.

Insects like weeds.

q

Plant a seed in a pot.

Check the lamps.
Do you need them on?

If you are keen to be green,
go down the street on two feet!